Anonymus

The Christmas bells

And their message; and other stories

Anonymus

The Christmas bells
And their message; and other stories

ISBN/EAN: 9783742835826

Manufactured in Europe, USA, Canada, Australia, Japa

Cover: Foto ©Andreas Hilbeck / pixelio.de

Manufactured and distributed by brebook publishing software (www.brebook.com)

Anonymus

The Christmas bells

"LET ME SEE 'EM," SAID HIS FATHER. [Page 109.]

The Christmas Bells

AND THEIR MESSAGE,

AND OTHER STORIES.

"Ring out, wild bells, to the wild sky."
                        Tennyson.

LONDON:
The Book Society, 28, Paternoster Row.

CONTENTS.

THE CHRISTMAS BELLS.

	PAGE
CHAPTER I.	
"Summat turns up"	7
CHAPTER II.	
The Man in the Wooden Box	17
CHAPTER III.	
The Story of Christmas-Eve	21
CHAPTER IV.	
Awakened by the "Angel"	31
CHAPTER V.	
The Song of the Bells	41
CHAPTER VI.	
Ned Learns the Meaning of the Song . . .	45
CHAPTER VII.	
Mary's Home	51
CHAPTER VIII.	
How Ned ate his Christmas Dinner	61

CONTENTS.

CHAPTER IX.
Mary falls among Friends 68

CHAPTER X.
How the Bells still Sing the same Song . . . 76

HOW THE UMBRELLA RAN AWAY WITH ELLIE 83

JACK'S CHRISTMAS 101

NO POCKET 121

THE CHRISTMAS BELLS

AND THEIR MESSAGE.

CHAPTER I.

"SUMMAT TURNS UP."

EVERY one seemed happy that Christmas-eve except Ned Black. All the shops were dressed out in Christmas costume: the greengrocers' set in a green frame of holly and laurels; the butchers' with prize meat in their windows; the poulterers' with turkeys and geese and hares covering all the outside of the shops; the grocers' with windows full of raisins and currants, and beautiful ornamental boxes of fruits; the book and toy shops full of brilliant novelties, as Christmas presents and New Year's gifts; and the sweet-shops vieing with all the rest in their wonderful treasures of Christmas-tree ornaments and decorations; while the oil and candle shops seemed changed into waxen temples, with their many-coloured columns of green, and red, and white, and orange candles, ranging in all sizes, from the tiniest dwarf to the most monstrous giant, with graceful festoons of green leaves and red berries chastening their glare. All within looked brilliant and warm; but outside, in the streets, above the glare of the gas-lamps, the far-off stars twinkled so brightly, and the air was so piercingly cold, that it was evident there was a hard frost.

"Fine seasonable weather!" "Regular Christmas weather!" were the often repeated remarks of one and another, as they met in the streets, after exchanging

the greeting, "A merry Christmas to you!"
—"The same to you."

"Merry Chris'mus indeed!" thought poor Ned Black to himself, as, with jacket much too small for him, buttonless, but fastened together with bits of string, and with trousers which let in the cold wind through large and ragged holes to his almost blue legs, he wandered up and down the streets, with bare feet, which shrank away from the frozen puddles on the pavement and in the road, and hands deep sunk in his pockets, trying to keep them warm. "Here's all on 'em talking 'bout a merry Chris'mus; and it's all wery well for them as 'as got 'omes and fires, and lots to eat and drink; but I don't see as it's wery merry for me." And thinking such thoughts, he often stopped outside some shop more brilliantly lighted than its neighbours, and tried to warm himself with the small quantity of heat diffused by the many gas-lights shining on and through the window-panes. "Merry Chris'mus! what's the good o' Chris'mus to me, I should like to know? Summer-time 't seems to me 's a deal more merrier, when its fine and 'ot, so as I can sleep out o' nights wi'out getting all perished wi' cold, and when I don't 'ave to spend nothink a-gettin' a lodgin', or else 'as to go into the *Workus*. And 'ere I've been all this 'ere day a-lookin' out for a job, and I can't get none nohows. A fine merry Chris'mus to such as me!—'aint it jest? And yet 'ere's all on 'em a'most a talkin' 'bout merry Chris'mus, and merry Chris'mus! I wish ther' was no Chris'mus at all— leastways now I do. It bean't like it used to was afore father died, and afore mother runned away and left me all alone. Used to like Chris'mus then, like other folks; but it bean't like them times now. Oh dear! oh dear!"

Such were the thoughts that kept flitting through poor Ned's mind as he went on and on, up and down the streets—to some so full of cheerfulness, to some how laden with misery!—still on the look-out for a job. Three years ago, his father, a blacksmith, hard working but utterly improvident, had died, leaving no means to support his widow and two children, who had thus been compelled to give up their home. Very soon the mother deserted them; and the two children, Ned and his little sister Mary, were left alone in the world, and without a friend. And yet not quite friendless. One of their father's old work-fellows, Jim Scroggs, and his wife, agreed to let little Mary Black live with them, and take care of their young children. Mary was only seven years old; and it was no easy life she had to live, with swearing, drunken Jim and his scolding wife, and with babies to look after, and nurse and carry by the hour together. But, at least, she was in a way provided for; and Ned had only to look after and take care of himself. This, for the three years which had elapsed since his father's death, he had contrived to do, until now, at the age of thirteen, he was wandering about the streets in utter poverty and rags, on this Christmas-eve. But if he had been asked *how* he had supported himself, he would have found it a hard task to say. By running errands; carrying bags and parcels from railway stations; selling matches; sweeping a crossing; and in various other ways by which it had been possible to earn a few coppers, he had managed to keep body and soul together, receiving occasional assistance from the Workhouse, especially in the winter-time. For the last few weeks he had been very badly off; and on the morning of this Christmas-eve he had left the lodging-house where he had passed the night, without a breakfast and without a half-penny. All day long he had been on the lookout for some means of earning a few pence, but in vain. All his efforts had been unavailing; and now the evening had come on, and he was beginning to think he would have, after all, to go into the Workhouse, unless "summat turns up" and he could get a job. Meantime he was obtaining what enjoyment he could from the *outside* of the shops, with limbs half frozen, and the gnawing pains of hunger, as his sole companions.

"A merry Christmas to you!" again sounded in his ears. Turning round from the window of a bookseller's shop, at the corner of a street, through which he had been looking with longing gaze at some large coloured pictures, Ned saw that the greeting was exchanged between two gentlemen who had just met; and he was watching them, thinking what it must be like to be merry, when he was nearly knocked over by a bluff, hearty, jolly-looking old gentleman, who, with parcels under his arms and in both hands, just then came out of the shop, and accidentally ran against him.

Ned reeled to the edge of the pavement, and, on recovering himself, was beginning to exclaim angrily against the gentleman who had so nearly knocked him down, when, seeing his opportunity, and how heavily the gentleman was laden, he curbed his rising anger, and " Carry 'em for yer, Sir? 'ere yer are, Sir," he began;

and, almost before the gentleman knew what he was doing, Ned had got about half-a-dozen packages into his keeping.

"Ah! but, my lad, you're too small," he said.

"No, I bean't, 'deed I bean't, Sir. I'll take 'em for yer, Sir, all right, Sir."

"But I've got about two miles to go: you'll never be able to carry them all that way. I must get a bigger boy, or have a cab."

"No, now don't yer go and do no sich thing, Sir—I'll take 'em, Sir; and the further 'tis, all the better, Sir, 'cos yer'll give me more for carryin' on 'em, Sir," said Ned; and his eyes twinkled with pleasure at the thought that he had got a job at last, and, after all, would not have to go to the Workhouse.

"Well, come along then," said the gentleman; "but mind you don't drop any of them. And be sure you don't try to run away, but keep close alongside of me; for if I catch you running off, I'll soon set the police after you."

"Dunno' fear, Sir; I'll come along all right, you'll see, Sir."

Keeping close at the gentleman's heels, with arms aching from the weight of the parcels, and the cold numbing his fingers, Ned trudged along, until at length they reached a large house, situated in a square about two miles off. The shutters were not closed; and through the deep crimson curtains before the parlour-windows there shone forth a bright red glow, which shed an appearance of warmth and comfort even to the outside. Ned had to wait till the door was opened, and the gentleman himself took the parcels from him to see if they were all right. Then, finding they were all quite safe, he asked how much he expected for the job.

"Leave it to you, Sir," said Ned; "but it's wery cold, Sir, and Chris'mus time, Sir, and I've 'ad nothink t' eat all day, Sir."

"Well, my boy, I should think sixpence will do, won't it?"

"Thank yer, Sir—yes, Sir," said Ned;

and then, remembering what he had heard repeated so often that evening, he added, "Merry Chris'mus, Sir!"

"The same to you, my boy," said the gentleman. "Here, wait a bit;" and feeling in his pockets, he pulled out all the coppers he could find in them, and gave them to Ned, in addition to the sixpence. There was threepence in all; and thus, with ninepence in his pocket, Ned ran away, richer and more happy by far than he had been for some days past.

CHAPTER II.

THE MAN IN THE WOODEN BOX.

AT the first baker's shop he came to, Ned bought a pennyworth of stale bread, and, munching it as he went along, he made his way back towards the streets he knew best, considering which lodging-house, of the many known to him, he would patronise that night, as now he could afford to pay his twopence for a bed. As he wandered on, suddenly, as he was passing a building standing in the middle of a terrace, having houses adjoining it on each side, he stopped; for he saw that the doors were open, and that inside the passage were

some inner red doors that looked warm,
and like the crimson curtains of the house
he had just left; and, coming through the
doorway, were sounds of music. These
strains it was that had first attracted his
attention. "Why shouldn't I 'ave a look
in?" said Ned to himself. Giving a quick
glance all round, he ran up the steps, and,
very quietly opening one of the red inner
doors, peeped in cautiously, ready to take
to his heels if he found he was observed.
He saw, a good way down a passage which
was covered with cocoa-nut matting, a
number of people sitting in wooden divi-
sions, which reminded him of the com-
partments in an eating-house he had sometimes been to; and, at the other end of
the building, he noticed a man, dressed up
in a queer cloak, inside a wooden box,
something like (Ned thought) the "Punch
and Judy" box, only this was all of wood,
and larger, and had stairs leading up to
a door near the top. He had entered a
chapel, in which, on this Christmas-eve,
service was being held; and the minister

had just given out a hymn; and it was the tune being played over on the organ, before the people began to sing, that had first made Ned stop and listen. As he still stood at the door, keeping it just ajar, that he might see what was going on, the organ ceased playing. It was very warm and comfortable inside; and outside the air was very cold and biting. Large hot pipes ran down the aisle; and the building was so beautifully decorated with holly and laurel, that Ned thought, if no one saw him, he might as well go in and listen for a bit, and see all that there was to be seen, and get warm. So when no one, as he thought, was looking—for all the people were at the pulpit end of the chapel—he slipped very quietly down the aisle, until he came to another aisle at right angles to the first, where he saw a form, and just by it a large coil of the hot pipes. Sitting down upon this form, in the shadow of a large stone pillar, Ned heard the man in the wooden box (for that was what he called the pulpit) begin to read. He was giving out again the first verse of the hymn—

> "Hark! the herald angels sing,
> Glory to the new-born King;
> Peace on earth, and mercy mild;
> God and sinners reconciled."

Immediately afterwards the people began to sing; and as they sang, Ned thought how beautiful the music was. Never before had he heard such a full depth of sweet tones: only in public-houses, and from bands and organs in the streets, and occasionally from a stray violin or concertina player in the poor lodging-houses he frequented, had music hitherto presented its charms to poor little Ned; and now he sat and listened, thoroughly delighted. Presently the music ceased, and all the people sat down, while Ned anxiously waited to see what was to come next.

CHAPTER III.

THE STORY OF CHRISTMAS-EVE.

AS Ned waited on, hoping that he would not have to go out again into the cold just yet, the man in the wooden box began to speak. After opening a large book that lay on a crimson velvet cushion before him, and reading a few words from it, he went on to talk; and for a little while Ned understood scarcely anything of what he said; but by-and-by he found himself listening to what seemed to him a wonderful story. Something like this were the words he heard:—

"There may seem no need, my friends, to tell again the oft-told tale of Christ's nativity, so well known to us all from our earliest childhood, and loved as long as known; and yet, on this Christmas-eve, I think it may possibly do none of us any harm once again to endeavour to picture to ourselves the touching scene. A calm, still night: stars glistening and twinkling in the full glory of that brightness which only an Eastern sky can show forth: the quiet, peaceful hill-sides, with their rich pasturage, overlooking vales more placid and peaceful still: at a little distance, the village of Bethlehem wrapped, with but a solitary exception, in almost perfect darkness and undisturbed repose: the white buildings of the Zion, beautiful for situation, the joy of the whole earth, scarce seen, and yet, because so dearly loved, to be perceived by loving eyes even in that subdued and tender light: the flocks of sheep penned up in sure keeping, safe from all harm: and the shepherds, clad in their flowing Eastern robes, reposing watchfully, in company, after their evening's toil; amid all the well-known beauties of the scene, perchance once again touched by its peacefulness, as they had been many a time before; and their hearts (may we not imagine?) under the sweet and soothing influence of that tenderly beautiful, trust-creating, trust-renewing national poem of theirs, 'The Lord my shepherd is; no want e'er shall I know,' —and thus their inmost being prepared, by communion with God through the works of His hands and the word of His servant, for that fuller revelation of the brightness of His glory,—for the dawning of that Sun of Righteousness, arising, even then, with healing in His wings— that celestial Light which was to eclipse— and yet to eclipse only by including within His purifying beams — all the myriad smaller lights under the whole heavens, kindled by those same far-reaching beams of His, to rule the night before His coming—lights sent by Him to represent Himself; to prepare the way for His dawning, by accustoming eyes, used too much to darkness, to the willing and joyful reception of His all-brightening rays—the rays of the perfectly pure white light of His eternal, His universal love.

"I like to think of the scene and the shepherds thus. An ideal picture, it may be said. If so, then well! May we, in that case, ourselves seek to rise to the highest ideal which we can imagine or desire may have been the shepherds' *real*, and so benefit even by what may be, after all, only an imaginary conception.

"And then the twilight of the star-light suddenly illuminated by a Presence awful in its purity—the Angel, with robe of such sparkling brightness as to seem to be composed of the sheen of the brightest of the stars, and yet with countenance more beautiful still, because lighted up *from within* by ineffable love. And then the clear silvery music—outvieing far the melodious rhythm of their psalm—of the Angelic Voice, as it trilled forth the message, re-assuring, and joy-inspiring, and catholic, and universal as God's own love, as God's own being—'Fear not!' and their troubled, anxious fears are all dispelled. 'For, behold, I bring you good tidings of great joy, which shall be to all people:' and a holy pulsation of joy, which they are glad to feel, rather than think, is *for all*, involuntarily almost, thrills through all their being (so, at least, I fain would think). 'For unto you is born this day, in the city of David, a Saviour, who is Christ the Lord.' 'Then, the good time *has* come in our day,' the thought darts with lightning speed, perchance, through the mind of one of them. 'But how shall we find Him? Where is He? Is it true? or can it be a dream?' And then the musical tones of the voice resume —for, indeed, they have scarcely ceased— 'And this shall be a sign unto you, Ye shall find the babe wrapped in swaddling clothes, lying in a manger.' And almost before their ears had received the last strange, seemingly contradictory words, or their hearts at all appreciated their significance, otherwise than by a startled chill of disappointment, suddenly all thoughts and feelings of their own are rapt away in awful wonder, as a ring of glorious ones, Angels, like the first, bursts in dazzling brilliancy into their view; while, with supreme delight, their ears are ravished with those strains—unearthly in their sweetness, and yet awe-inspiring in their grandeur—tones the most beautiful of their kind our world has ever heard—'peace on earth, goodwill toward men.' And then a disappearance as sudden as their advent. The silent stars resume their former watch. The hill-sides are peacefully calm and quiet as before. Again the far-off gleams of the buildings of Jerusalem shine forth faintly in the starlight. Again the hush of night is undisturbed. The flocks are still in their folds. But in the hearts of those poor men all is changed. There has dawned upon their souls a glimpse of eternal beauty. There have been inbreathed into their hearts a hope for all mankind, which shall never die; a new life-spirit of brotherly love, resulting from the glimpse they have had of God's love to them; a feeling of peace, deeper and more joyful than that which possessed them before.

"And then, by common consent, leaving their flocks upon the hill-side, they make their way along the oft-trodden path leading down to Bethlehem, nothing doubting that what the Angel had made known to them their eyes should see. And as they reach the village—usually so quiet, but which had been that day the scene of so much bustle and traffic, occasioned by the arrival of so many strangers, and which had now again sunk into its accustomed stillness—they walk along, looking eagerly for any sign of wakefulness in the inhabitants of the houses which line the way until they reach the Caravanserai—the strangers' tarrying-place. Entering it noiselessly, they pass amidst the sleeping travellers, until, in a secluded nook, they find the new-made mother, with her husband and *the* Babe. Could it be that this little infant was the Saviour, of whom the

Angel had spoken? Yes, they believe He is. The Angel's story has left no room for doubts in their minds; and, telling their own marvellous tale, they presently return, publishing abroad the story, that others too may share the blessedness of knowing what they know about the Saviour-Child Jesus—return, glorifying and praising God.

"This is, perhaps, very much a fancy picture. Merely the outlines of the story have been drawn for us; and, if we would try to realize the event as it happened, we must fill in the details as best we can; and so long as each one who attempts the task does so in a loving, reverent spirit, it matters little how many different imaginative pictures may be sketched. But let us not forget the meaning of it all:—'God so loved the world, as to give His only Son.' A loving Giver; a willing, self-sacrificing Gift! 'Lo! I come, I delight to do Thy will.' The Christmas message is, indeed, a message of Love—from God, who is Love—by Jesus, who is Love—to man, the deep need of whose heart is Love, and the effect of the reception of which is love—love to God and love to man. Brethren, if God so loved us, we ought also to love one another. Thus, as the result of the Christmas story, I ask you all to bear in memory what Christmas means. It means that Jesus loves us; it means, we must love one another. And if this Christmas spirit be shed abroad in our hearts, we shall have what I sincerely hope you all may have, a happy, loving Christmas—a really merry Christmas. May God grant to us all to have such an one! Amen."

Poor Ned rubbed his eyes. "'Ave I been to sleep," he thought, "and been a-dreaming? Where am I?" He looked up, and found that again some words were being read. The organ began to play, and soon the people joined in the singing. And now, at length, Ned—who, amidst all that the minister had said in his short sermon, had comprehended little more than that the man in the wooden box had been "telling a rare an' fine story," and had ended by saying that Jesus loves us, and that we are to love one another, and had wished every one a "Merry Chris'mus"—worn out by fatigue, and overcome by the warmth of the pipes, dropped fast off to sleep.

CHAPTER IV.

AWAKENED BY THE "ANGEL."

PRESENTLY he was awakened by some one shaking him gently by the arm. He rubbed his eyes, and looked about him. The lights were almost all out in the chapel; the people had all gone; the wooden box was empty; all was hushed and still. Standing before him was the minister, divested now of his gown, but easily recognised by Ned as the man whom he had seen in the wooden box; and with him there was a most beautiful little girl, whom Ned, in his half-waking, half-sleeping state, confused in his mind with the Angel of whom he had been hearing or dreaming—which of the two he hardly knew. With long, wavy, flaxen hair flowing unrestrainedly over her shoulders, her eyes, in the now dim light, almost sparkling in their brightness, and yet looking with so much of pity at the poor, ragged, barefooted boy, little Alice Wills might well have been mistaken even by better-informed people than poor Ned, for one of the celestial throng, looking, as she did, like a ministering spirit, sent forth, as an angel, a messenger of love, by her Father, to minister in love.

Mr. Wills, the minister, had, from his pulpit, noticed poor little Ned enter the chapel, and, with a half-frightened look, creep up the aisle, and at length shelter himself behind the stone pillar. As the sermon proceeded, he often looked down, but at first could not see him; but presently the ragged boy, intent upon hearing the story, leaned forward, and the minister perceived how eagerly he was listening; until, at its close, when the concluding hymn was being sung, he saw Ned leaning apparently fast asleep, against the pillar. After the service was over, and many friendly Christmas greetings had been exchanged, the minister retired into his vestry, where he was soon joined by his little motherless girl; and he determined that as he went out, he would see whether the poor boy was still there, and, if so, that he would try to learn something about him. Thus it was that Ned, who had escaped the observation of all the congregation, as they passed out down the main aisles, and had not even, as yet, been perceived by the pew-opener, who was turning out the gas, was suddenly awakened by the minister giving him a gentle shake, all his efforts to rouse him by speaking having proved ineffectual.

Upon recognising the minister, Ned felt somewhat reassured. He began to get up; but, utterly tired out, and at first not completely aroused from his sleep, he sank down again upon the seat, staring at the minister, and wondering what was to come next.

"Well, my poor boy, what are you doing here?" asked the minister. "Don't you see every one else has gone, and the chapel is going to be locked up?"

"Didn't mean no 'arm, Sir," said Ned, "and I'll be off d'rec'ly, Sir; 'ope you won't give me in charge, Sir. I ain't done no 'arm, 'deed, Sir, nor tooked nothink, Sir."

"How did you happen to come here, my boy?" asked Mr. Wills; "where do you live?"

"I don't live nowheres, Sir—not reg'lar, Sir; I gets a lodgin' when I can, Sir, but oftener nor not I sleeps under a cart, or in a stable, or a cab, or a shed, or a shutter-box, Sir. I ain't got no 'ome, Sir, and it's bitter an' cold, Sir, o' nights now, Sir; and two or three times I've been to the Workus for a bit, when it's wery wet and cold, Sir."

"Haven't you any father or mother, my poor boy, or any friends who look after you?"

"No, Sir, ne'er a one, Sir. Father's dead, and mother's runned away; and I ain't got no friends at all now, 'cept little

Mary—she's my sister, Sir,—but she don't live along o' me. She keeps at Master Scroggs's, to mind the babies, she does; and there's allus a lot of babies there, and they don't like me for to go and see her."

"What do you do for a living, then, my lad?"

"Anythink as I can, Sir. 'Times I sells matches, and 'times I sells things in the streets—but then the p'lice comes arter us, and drives us away,—and 'times I runs errands, or carries bags and pockmanters at the rail'ays, or opens cab doors; and oncet, for a good long spell, I 'ad a crossin', Sir—a genelman he guv me a broom, Sir, but the broom wored itself out, and a big feller he comed and tooked my crossin' away from me, and so I've been a-lookin' out for jobs at the rail'ay stations most o' late, Sir."

"But what made you come in here, my boy?"

"Well, Sir, I'd a been a-waitin' all day for a job, Sir, and I 'adn't 'ad nothink t' eat since last night, Sir, and I couldn't get nothink to do, and I was a-thinkin' as 'ow I'd 'ave to go into the Workus again, Sir; but I thought as 'ow I'd 'ave a good look at all the fine things in the shops fust; and as I was a-goin' along, a genelman knocked me over a'most, and he'd got lot's o' parcels, and he give 'em to me to carry 'em; and, arter he'd paid me, I bought a bit o' bread, and I was a-goin' along back again, thinkin' as 'ow I'd go afore long and get a night's lodgin' as I knows on, where I could 'ave a good long time along o' the fire—for I was awful an' cold, Sir,—when I 'eerd the music in 'ere, Sir, and I looked in through one of them 'ere red doors, Sir, and it was so fine an' warm as I thought 'twouldn't be a-doin' no one's any 'arm if I war to stay a bit; and so I comed in, and 'eerd the singin' and you a-tellin' that 'ere story, Sir; and I'd a been so cold all day, Sir, and when I got along 'o these 'ere hot pipes, I s'pose it made me go asleep; and that's 'ow it was, Sir. But I'll be off this minute now, 'deed I will, Sir;" and poor little Ned took his bare chilblained feet off the bottom pipe, upon which he had been resting them, and, treading on the cold stone passage, rose up to go.

But Alice Wills had been listening to his tale with a heart melting with pity for the poor homeless, ragged boy; and the spirit of Christmas time, and her father's description of the story of that wonderful love in Bethlehem long ago, had made her especially sensitive to any claims upon her compassion.

"O papa! don't let him go yet; do stop him. We won't do you any harm, little boy; do wait. Papa, mayn't he come to our children's Christmas dinner to-morrow? He's so poor, and he's just one of those we wanted to help so much!—do please let him come, papa. Look, he's got no shoes on, and his clothes are so ragged and thin. He may come, mayn't he?"

"Yes, dear, I shall be very glad for him to come. I think he's honest, and has been telling the truth. And whether or no, if Jesus were living amongst us now,

I think he is one of the poor lost ones whom He would have been sure to seek out and save; and we'll believe—won't we, Alice?—that Jesus sent him in here that we might help him to have a happy Christmas."

"Oh, yes; and thank you so much, dear papa. I have got a ticket here;" and opening her purse, she took from it a blue card; and telling him to come on the morrow, at two o'clock, to the school just round the corner of the terrace in Albemarle Street, and to be sure not to lose the ticket, but to bring it with him, she gave it to him. Then, seeing how very thin and white his hands were, and how extremely poor he looked, she took out from her purse a bright new shilling—all the money she possessed—and, after hesitating an instant, slipped that too into his hand.

"And now, my poor boy, come along," said the minister; "we must all go home. I hope you'll remember what I have been telling you—my Christmas-eve story—and that you may have a merry Christmas."

They soon reached the door; and great was the astonishment of the pew-opener, and many were her exclamations of surprise, to see, with the minister and his little girl, the ragged, barefooted little boy, whom she had not seen until now. "Well, to be sure! and what's the minister up to now?" she exclaimed; "and whatever will he go and do next?—encouraging a dirty little chap like that in the chapel! and just after I've swept up all the evergreens and rubbish, and made it all neat and clean for to-morrow. How ever he came in passes my comprehension; and me never to have seen him till this blessed minute! I shouldn't wonder if he hasn't been a-hiding away ever since I went to tea, and left all them laughing, careless girls in the place, a' purpose to steal the books." And, with anything but a benediction in her looks, she let the three out; but, standing in a great deal of awe of the minister, her feelings of astonishment and suspicion were expressed in too low a tone to reach his ears.

When they reached the street, Alice turned to Ned :—" Good-bye, little boy : don't forget to come to-morrow—at two o'clock, recollect. I shall look out for you, and keep you a place at my table. But we don't know his name, papa. What is your name ?"

" Ned Black ; but most on 'em only calls me Ned, when they calls me onythink at all."

" Well, *Ned*, then, good night, and a merry Christmas ; and don't forget to-morrow."

And then they left him—left him bewildered, and wondering what it all meant ; till, feeling the ticket and the shilling in his hand, he put them safely away in his trousers-pocket, with the eightpence that still remained after buying the bread ; and, with his hands in his pockets, and constantly feeling to see if his treasures were all safe, he set off down the brightly lighted streets towards the lodging-house where he intended to sleep.

CHAPTER V.

THE SONG OF THE BELLS.

"ERRY Chris'mus!" Ned said to himself, as he walked along. "*She* wished me a merry Chris'mus. I do b'lieve I shall 'ave un, arter all, now. Won't it be jolly an' fine t' 'ave a real good Chris'mus dinner tomorrer! I ain't 'ad a downright good dinner no more nor twice since father died. And 'ow kind she was, and real beautiful! She must be like them 'ere Angels her father's been a-tellin' that 'ere story 'bout. 'Spects, if I lived long o' her,

'twouldn't be so diff'cult to be a bit betterer."

Just then the Bells of a church close by began to ring merrily out in the clear frosty air. Ned stopped to listen; and as he listened, the rhythm of the Bells seemed to form itself into words. Where they came from Ned did not know; but the story, and the sermon, and the hymn that he had heard sung in the chapel, and the musical ring of the Bells, and (may we not believe?) the inspiration of the Most High, who bears on His heart of love the lowliest of mankind, all united together to help, and, to Ned, the Bells distinctly chimed—

"Love one another!
Jesus loves you;
Love one another!
Love Jesus too!"

Ned repeated them over again and again to himself, and the simple words seemed each time to fall in with the cadence of the Bells—

" Love one another!
Jesus loves you;

Love one another!
Love Jesus too!"

And Ned, glad at heart,—but hardly knowing why he was so glad, for it was not merely owing to his good fortune, but the very spirit of the Christmas season seemed, with the voices of the Bells, to have entered into his heart—a sense of the love of Jesus to him, even him, poor friendless Ned Black, inspiring him to seek to love some one else, and "Jesus too,"—wandered along, staying in the streets much longer than he had intended, but led along from one peal of Church Bells to another by the desire to see if they would all sing the same song. And to Ned, now carrying the idea of the words to them, and seeking to fit them to the varying chimes, it really appeared as if they all repeated the same words—

"Love one another!
Jesus loves you;
Love one another!
Love Jesus too!"

At length, completely tired out, he

treated himself to some hot baked potatoes and a penny currant roll for his supper, and went to seek his bed; but all through the night he was dreaming of the song of the *Christmas Bells.*

CHAPTER VI.

NED LEARNS THE MEANING OF THE SONG.

THE next morning he was awakened by a neighbouring clock striking eight; and as he lay and counted the strokes, again, to welcome in the merry Christmas morning, rang out the joyful peal of the Bells, and again to Ned their oft-repeated message was the same. He got up, and went down to a pump in the court; and, notwithstanding that there was still a hard frost, he gave himself a good sluicing, and then went in to thaw his half-numbed toes and fingers at the common fire. As he sat there, he heard the bells clang out once more, and their message set him thinking :—

"S'pose I tried to do what the Bells say, and what the man as told the story talked on last night, *I* ain't got nobody t' love, and there bean't nobody to love me;" but just at that moment he caught himself repeating the second line of the chant of the Bells,—"*Jesus* loves you." "I wonner if it's true that He does love me!" thought Ned. "Don't look much like 't in gen'ral. I ain't 'ad no new clo'es for I donno 'ow long; and I'm allers a'most out in th' cold, and wind, and rain, and I'm more oftener 'ungry nor not; and nobody don't care for me, or speaks kind to me; and I ain't got no 'ome. Don't look much like as if Jesus, nor no one else, did care for the likes o' me, whativer He does t' other folks; and most on 'em does seem a deal betterer off nor I—though *I* don't see what Jesus, if him's the same as the genelman talked about last night, 'as to do with ony on us; *I* knows *I* never see'd Him, nor no angels, nor nothink, as ever *I* 'members;"

and Ned, after the excitement of the previous evening, was getting into a very unChristmaslike state of despondency, when, taking his right hand away from the fire, and thrusting it into his pocket, it came in contact with his money and the dinnerticket, both of which he had for the moment forgotten. And the Bells pealed obstinately forth, after two or three rounds, as though determined that they were right, and that they would have their own way, the message of the second line again, "Jesus loves *you*," so that the events of the preceding evening flowed back in full tide upon his memory.

He thought of the little girl, and her kindness to him; of her gift of the new shilling, and of her invitation to the dinner; and then he remembered, for the first time, her having said that it must have been Jesus who had sent him there; and he tried, but quite unsuccessfully, to understand how He could have done so without his having seen Him, although he believed it must really have been the case, as the little girl seemed so sure of it. "But I don't rec'lect nothink 'bout it," thought Ned. Then he endeavoured to recall as much as he could of the minister's Christmas story; and, though he understood but little of the meaning of what had been said, the real heart of the meaning—the pitying love of the great God in becoming a little child for our sakes—had entered into his understanding through his heart (and what highest truths do not do so—are *not* hearttruths?) in such a way that when, after a pause, he heard the Bells chime forth anew, he listened to their ringing, rejoicing to hear the second line once more, "Jesus loves you;" and so, in his own poor, but true, and heartfelt, and trustful way, he set to his seal that God was true.

What should he do with himself that Christmas-day? How should he spend it so as to be most happy? Whom had *he* got to love?

Suddenly the thought of his little sister Mary entered his mind. "I ain't seen Mary not for ever so many months. Last time as I went, Jim Scroggs 'ad been out a-drinkin' all th' night afore, and he druv me away, and told me he'd break every bone in my body if I comed a-bothering of 'im again for ever sich a while; and so I ain't been not since then. I'm a good mind to go to-day, as it's Chris'mus-day. I'd like to see Mary very much, I would. I wonner 'ow she gets along with them Scroggses! she's worse off a deal nor me, after all—a-nussing all them babies, and bein' knocked about and scolded by Missus Scroggs—and can't she scold and 'it 'ard, too, jest!—and never bein' able to run about, or go out, when she wants to."

The bells struck in just then—or rather they again attracted his attention, for they had been ringing all the while—

> " Love one another!
> Jesus loves you;
> Love one another!
> Love Jesus too!

"Yes, I *will* go and see Mary, that I will; and I'll give her the sixpence I've got left out o' what the genelman guv me for the job last night, and I'll keep the rest o' what's left for myself. I'll try to love her to-day." And I think, although no prayer was uttered, Jesus took the *wish* for a prayer, and helped him to succeed.

He ran out and bought a pennyworth of bread at a baker's near, and so had to change his bright new shilling. This he was able to make into toast at the lodging-house fire; and, with water from the pump in the yard, he made a hearty breakfast. Then he sallied out for the day.

CHAPTER VII.

MARY'S HOME.

THE sun was shining brightly, and it was a fine, cheery, frosty Christmas morning, as Ned left the lodging-house. After a while he met a great many persons going to church and chapel, and he had a good mind to try and go himself. With this half-formed purpose, he found his way to the chapel where he had been the preceding evening, and lingered about on the opposite side of the way irresolutely, hoping he might see his friends, the minister and little Alice, without being himself perceived. And, by-and-by, his patience was rewarded. Mr.

Wills and his light-haired little daughter
(who Ned now noticed was dressed
wholly in black) came down the street,
and, meeting some friends at the door,
they all entered the building together.
Ned still waited on, hoping some opportunity might offer itself of his slipping in
unobserved; but so many persons—well
dressed most of them were, too—kept
entering the chapel, that he sorrowfully
determined it would never do for him to
go in, as he would be sure to be seen, and
stared at as an intruder, even if the pew-
opener—of whose black looks the night
before he retained a vivid recollection—
did not turn him out, and possibly give
him in charge. This latter alternative he
dreaded above everything, as poor Ned, in
the three years which had elapsed since he
had been thrown upon the world to take
care of himself, had more than once fallen
into the hands of the police for petty
thefts; and if he had been quite candid in
the enumeration of the various means by
which he had supported himself that he

had made to the minister, he would have been compelled to include many a meal bought with stolen money, and on one occasion, amongst his various lodgings, a month's imprisonment in the House of Correction. With the fear of again getting into the clutches of the police, and thus lose his dinner, and a real desire never to merit their attentions, he was turning away disappointed, when, just at that instant, the bells of a neighbouring church, at which the hour for commencing the service was later, pealed forth so merrily—

"Love one another!
Jesus loves you;
Love one another!
Love Jesus, too!"

that they reminded Ned of what he had almost forgotten—that he was going to see his little sister Mary.

Running with all his might to get warm —for he had become thoroughly chilled whilst waiting outside the chapel—he soon arrived at the court where Jim Scroggs lived. Notwithstanding the cold weather, the door of the house was open. Peeping round the corner of the door, Ned carefully reconnoitred the ground to ascertain whether Jim was in, and to get an idea as to the state of matters inside. Standing at a table in the middle of the room was Mrs. Scroggs, busily engaged in ironing some clothes. The room was in great confusion, and very dirty and uncomfortable. The breakfast-things had been put aside unwashed on a chest of drawers, which had become the temporary receptacle of a very motley group of articles, including a saucepan, and a kettle blackened by the fire, in close proximity to some faded finery which had been turned out of the still open drawers. A chair, which had lost one of its legs, had fallen over on its side close by; whilst another chair held a basin of dirty water. Rags and paper had been stuffed into several broken panes of glass in the small window, which thus afforded even less light than it had been intended to give. Under the stairs, which immediately faced the front door, and which led to a part of the house inhabited by another set of occupants, was the store of coals, which, as it had been recently replenished, strayed beyond its proper limits, making a litter of pieces of coal and small dust upon the floor. Altogether, the aspect of affairs was extremely wretched and uncomfortable. The only thing which brightened the gloom, and gave a look of home to the miserable dwelling, was a bright, cheerful fire, round which Ned saw seated his little sister Mary, with a big baby on her lap, and three other children. For the little children, who are ever the rays of light and love from God's own heart—the heart of the Father—to the hearts of his poorest and most sinful children, had not failed in their God-given message even here, in this abode of wretchedness, and poverty, and vice. Even here they were evidently loved and cared for after a fashion, and they shed forth a feeling of home about the place, which even poor drunken Jim, in his sober times, could not fail to appreciate. But such a time it was not now. It was Christmas; and therefore it was only fit, thought Jim, that he should "treat" himself. He had been out drinking the evening before, and had gone out again early this morning "on the spree," to find some public-house, where, although it was church-time, he might be able to get some beer. Encouraged by not seeing him, Ned entered, determining to be specially civil to Mrs. Scroggs—who, however, as he soon found, was not in the best of humours, on account of her husband's conduct—and thus to make good his position.

"Good morning, mum! merry Chris'mus to yer, mum!" he began. "May I come in and stay a bit, please, along o' Mary and the children?"

"Well, as it's Christmas-day, pr'aps you may for a while, so long as you keep out o' my way and don't teaze the children; but I can't be hindered, and I'm not a-going to be, nohows, for I've got a sight of ironing to do afore the afternoon, when I'm a-going out to tea along o' my sister. So go and sit down by the fire with the children, and help to keep 'em quiet, if you can."

"Thank-yer, mum; all right, mum; I'll be quiet and keep out o' yer way, you'll see."

And fearing the permission might be recalled, he made the best of his way through the midst of the children, and giving Mary a kiss, sat himself down on the floor by her side, taking the precaution to keep her between Mrs. Scroggs and himself. Very soon he and Mary were deep in mutual confidences; and Ned began to tell her his last night's experiences, which were fresh in his memory. Putting his hand in his pocket, he brought it out with his two sixpences clasped tightly within it, and told Mary to guess what he had got. Mary guessed buttons, a top, a whistle, a "cat," halfpence, and various other things, until she gave up in despair of being right. In great glee at her want of success, Ned at length opened his hand, and showed them to her.

"I thought as 'ow you'd never guess

right. Ain't it fine, Mary? I ain't been so rich not for ever so long. And, Mary," he continued, after looking to see that Mrs. Scroggs was not within hearing, "you'd never guess again, I'm sure, what I'm a-goin' to do with one on 'em. One on 'em's for you, Mary; I'm a-goin' to give it to you for your own, 'cos it's Chris'mus."

"Oh, Ned! you don't mean to say you'll give me one—not one of these sixpences for my very own? You can't mean it—do you really?"

"Yes, Mary, you're to 'ave one o' these, you are, indeed; and I am 'a-goin' to 'ave t'other. Which on 'em will you choose?"

"Oh, Ned! I don't know which; you are *so* kind. Thank you, dear Ned, oh, so much!" and little Mary threw her arms round Ned's neck, and kissed him again and again, while some happy tears rolled down her cheeks. Very little love had poor Mary known for the last three years since she had lived with the Scroggses, and Ned's unwonted kindness completely melted her.

Sixpence to her was a fortune; a penny suggested wonderful possibilities in the way of purchases. The last time that she had had any money of her own, was when Jim in a sudden fit of generosity gave her threepence to buy sweets with for herself and the children. With Ned's help it was speedily spent, and when Jim in the evening wanted even that little gift back, he found it had already gone down the children's throats, almost as rapidly as it would have rushed down his own.

CHAPTER VIII.

HOW NED ATE HIS CHRISTMAS DINNER.

HE Christmas services were over, and again a peal of Bells rang merrily out; and to Ned they still carried the same message, only this time it seemed a still more gladsome one than before. For he had tasted something now of the happiness that springs from unselfish well-doing; he had found out, by his own experience, the truth of words he had probably never heard—" It is more blessed to give than to receive;" and this result of attending to the Song of the Bells made him wish, listening as he was all the time to their chiming, to do something more,

that his pale little sister might have a really merry Christmas.

A sudden thought struck him. It was one o'clock, and at two he was to go with his ticket to the Christmas dinner at the schools. How would it do to let Mary go to the dinner instead of himself? No, he could not do that. No one could expect him to do that. But if he *did* make up his mind to let her go, would she be able to get in? But it did not matter—he must go himself. Yet he would have a look at the ticket, and see what it said. He drew it from his pocket, and began to read what was printed upon it. He had never quite lost the faculty of reading a little, which he had acquired when, in his father's lifetime, he had been to school for a short time; and now, with some difficulty, he spelt out the words, "Admit the Bearer." Yes, Mary could go. He understood the words enough to see that. But could he let her? He had been looking forward all day so much to going, and he should be so terribly disappointed to miss it after all.

But then, how very much Mary would enjoy it! he thought, and *he* was a boy, and older than his sister; he could be brave enough to bear up under a disappointment. He was sure he could be brave enough, if he really tried hard. He had a great mind to try. And then the story of the night before, and the thought of the good Son of God giving up His own pleasure—so Ned put it in his thoughts, not knowing that the Self-Sacrifice of Jesus, although such real self-sacrifice, was yet His supremest happiness—and giving it up, as the minister had said, for *him*, made Ned wish very much to do this for Mary. And the Bells decided the matter, putting an end to the conflict in his mind.

"Love one another!
Jesus loves you;
Love one another!
Love Jesus too!"

they seemed to repeat all the more clearly out of the silence which had been maintained whilst he had been pondering the reasons for, and against, her going.

"Yes, she shall go!" he suddenly burst out, as the Bells ceased their chiming. "Look 'ere, Mary, you'd like to go to th' dinner they're a-goin' to give to all on 'em this arternoon, wouldn't yer now? and I'm a-goin' to get you in; you're to 'ave my ticket, and then they'll let yer in right enough."

"Oh but, Ned, you're going yourself."

"No, I ain't: I mean 't let you go i'stid."

"But you can't mean it, Ned—do you really?" she repeated; until being assured again and again that Ned was in earnest, and did intend her to go, and that he would not be persuaded to alter his mind and go himself, she loaded him with kisses once more.

"Oh, thank you dear Ned, thank you so much; it is so very good of you. But I forgot; I'm afraid Mrs. Scroggs won't let me go after all; there'll be no one to mind the baby, or look after the children."

"I'll ask her t' let me stay the arternoon,

and nuss the baby while you're gone," said Ned.

So when Mrs. Scroggs re-entered the room, in a better temper now from having finished her ironing, and was standing over the fire watching the pot boil, in which were some bacon and potatoes for their dinner, Ned told his tale. By promising to stay with the children, and keep them quiet and out of mischief, he at length prevailed upon her to consent to Mary's going, and even to allow him to accompany her, to show her the way, upon his undertaking to make great haste back.

Much to Mary's delight it was settled; and, after a good wash, she put on her best frock, and while the children and Mrs. Scroggs were having their dinner, she went with Ned to the school. Instead of going up to the door, as he feared he might be seen by the minister or little Alice, Ned loitered about at a short distance from the entrance, until he saw Mary give up her ticket and enter. Then, having ascertained that the change in its ownership had not been discovered, he ran back as fast as he could; and, spending a penny upon some sweets to console himself, and help him in managing the children during the afternoon, he soon reached the Scroggses' house. Fortunately he was back before Mrs. Scroggs had expected him; and as the dinner-things were still upon the table, she heaped the leavings of the potatoes and bacon upon a plate, and, bidding him take the baby, and sit down by the fire, she left him to make what, to Ned, was a very good dinner. He had soon finished it, however, and then, getting the children close around him, he set to work to try to amuse them. By-and-by he got so interested himself in his novel employment, that, with an occasional resort to the little bag of sweets, and by the assistance of the children's broken toys, the afternoon passed rapidly away. But, in spite of his playing with the children, it did not pass without two or three short intervals occupied in wondering how Mary was getting on, and what she was doing, which grew into a longing that he had gone himself. Once during the afternoon this desire was growing so strong, and the feeling of disappointment so great, that had not the baby just then begun to cry, taking all Ned's care to coax and hush it off to sleep again, his own tears might have flowed instead. But when the baby was fairly asleep, bravely crushing down his feelings of trouble, he began repeating, first to himself, and after awhile aloud to the children, the Bells' message, until he had taught them to join him in trying to sing its song—

> "Love one another!
> Jesus loves you;
> Love one another!
> Love Jesus too!"

So he conquered his disappointment, and the afternoon wore speedily away.

CHAPTER IX.

MARY FALLS AMONG FRIENDS.

SOON it became quite dark outside; and, within, the room was lit up only by the firelight. Queer shadows were dancing on the walls, and Ned and the children were trying to make with their hands the funniest shadows they could produce. Mrs. Scroggs was in the back room getting ready to go out. Suddenly, the door opened, and, to Ned's extreme surprise, who should enter, but, as he first thought, as the firelight gleamed upon her golden hair, the Angel of the Christmas-eve story. But this idea held possession of his mind for an instant only; for the light grew brighter, and he recognised immediately little Alice Wills, who entered the room, holding Mary by the hand, while behind, stood the minister, Mr. Wills, himself. To account for their appearance, it is necessary to go back a little in our story.

When Mary entered the schoolroom, she was passed on, with a number of other girls, to the top of the large room, and there seated at a long table, covered with a clean white cloth, upon which knives and forks and spoons were arranged. At first she felt very strange and uncomfortable; but soon a little girl, very clean and neat in her dress (which, with the exception of a spotlessly white pinafore, was wholly black), who was seated next to her, began to talk, and Mary at once felt she had found a friend. When the boys had all entered, and had taken their places at a similar table at the other end of the room, a bell was struck, and when silence was obtained, the minister spoke a few words of welcome, wishing them all a very merry Christmas. Then he gave out a grace which the children sang, and then the dinner began. A number of young ladies handed round to the children plates of roast beef and vegetables, as fast as the gentlemen who had come to help could serve them. Assuredly to the helpers it was a truly merry Christmas-time; they seemed to enjoy the waiting, as much as, if not more than, the hungry children did the feast which was so bountifully supplied to them; they, too, "tasting the joy of doing kindnesses."

Then followed the pudding, or, rather, the many puddings, brought in smoking hot, each with a sprig of holly stuck in the top. Soon the empty dishes bore testimony to their popularity. But, although the children tried hard to exhaust the supply, their efforts were unsuccessful: all had as much as they could eat, and yet there was still to spare.

Little Alice Wills had chosen that part of the girls' table to wait at, where Mary and her new-found friend in the black dress were sitting. Mary soon discovered that her name was Jessie Simpson, and that her mother had died not long before. She told Mary, too, that she went regularly every Sunday to the Sunday-school, and that she and Alice Wills were in the same class; and that they were great friends. Indeed, it was for the pleasure of being near to Jessie that Alice had selected that part of the table to wait at. After the boys had been admitted, Alice had walked all round the table where they were seated, hoping to find and speak a word of welcome to poor Ned. But, of course, she had been unable to find him. She was a good deal disappointed; for she had been looking forward with much pleasure to the delight she would have in welcoming, and attending to, her own special guest, and in seeing him thoroughly enjoy himself. But, in the excitement of the dinner, all such thoughts speedily disappeared; and when it was finished, she found room, and came and sat down by Jessie's side at the table.

Then, for the first time, little Mary Black attracted her special attention. Asking who she was, and where she lived, her kind inquiries soon elicited from Mary her story, and the fact that it was in consequence of Ned's having given her his ticket that she came to be there at all. This, then, explained his unaccountable absence.

Springing from her seat, Alice ran up to her father, and, bringing him with all the speed she could to the table, she told him about Ned's generosity to his little sister, and his unselfish kindness; and then Mr. Wills, who was very kind and gentle, heard over again from her own lips Mary's story of Ned's goodness to her. For, in spite of her shyness usually with strangers, to-day, as soon as she began to talk about Ned, she forgot herself in her subject.

"Oh, papa, wasn't it good of Ned? what can we do for him?" exclaimed Alice, when Mary had finished her tale for the second time. "I don't think I could have done so, if I had been as poor and hungry as he looked last night. Wasn't it good?"

"Indeed it was, Alice dear—indeed it was. We must see what we can do for him, although anything that we can do is likely to fall short of his own generous kindness to his poor little sister."

Then turning to Mary, he asked more particularly where she lived, and whether Ned would be still waiting for her; and, hearing he was to stay at Mrs. Scroggs's until Mary's return, he told her to wait behind when the other children were sent home.

Returning to the desk, he gave out another grace, which the children sang. And then he began to speak to them; not giving them anything like a formal address, but telling them two or three simple stories, thoroughly gaining their attention, and awakening their interest. And, at the close, he told them the Christmas story of Bethlehem, in simple, childly language; concluding with a few words of prayer, in which he asked that the Christmas spirit of love—the love made known and brought home to them in the earthly life of their loving Friend and Saviour, Jesus—might influence all their hearts, all through their earthly lives, and so make them ready for His Home of love above. Then the Christmas hymn, "Hark! the Herald Angels sing," was sung, and the children were dismissed.

When every one else had gone, Mr. Wills, with Alice, and Mary Black, started to go to Mrs. Scroggs's. They reached the house after about a quarter of an hour's walk, and it was their entrance into the fire-lit room that had so astonished Ned. But more astonished still was he, when he discovered that Mary had told all about him to little Alice and her father, and at the praise which both gave him for his self-denying love. But what surprised him most of all, on afterwards thinking over what had happened, was that, as he sat in the firelight upon the floor, by Alice's side, and as she bent over him and talked to him, she so won his confidence by her loveliness and gentle kindness, that before long he had told her all about the Bells, and the song they had sung to him—

> " Love one another!
> Jesus loves you;
> Love one another!
> Love Jesus too!"

and how it was owing to their influence that he had acted as he had done.

CHAPTER X.

HOW THE BELLS STILL SING THE SAME SONG.

WHEN Mr. Wills and Alice went home, to be present at their own Christmas family gathering, they took Ned with them; and after he had had a good wash, and put on some clothes which once belonged to a poor lad who had been errand-boy at Mr. Wills's, and had died not long before, he was sent into the kitchen, where, after a hearty dinner with the servants, the evening passed merrily away.

After dinner, Alice made it her urgent

request to her father that Ned might be engaged to clean the knives and boots, and be their errand-boy; and her father consented, arranging also that he should live in the house.

By industry, and by service always yielded willingly and cheerfully, because gratefully and lovingly, and accepted in a kindly, forbearing spirit, Ned prospered in his new place. Alice herself taught him to read and to write; and, above all, she told him about the loving Saviour; and Ned, who knew *she* was kind and good, and willing and anxious to help him in any way she could, was led, through the human love and sympathy, up to a fuller belief in, and reception of, the Divinely-Human love and sympathy and helpfulness of God Himself.

Thus, time passed rapidly away, and Ned kept his place in Mr. Wills's family for many a year. And every Christmas, as it came round, the Bells seemed to him to ring out the same old tune, with the same sweet message as of old, except that, every year, it grew sweeter and dearer—

>"Love one another!
>Jesus loves you;
>Love one another!
>Love Jesus too!"

And when, some years afterwards, upon the morning of a bright Christmas-day, little Alice Wills, who had grown into a true good woman, and become more beautiful than ever, was married, in a little country village Chapel, to the master of a large boys' school, Ned was present. And when, after the wedding, the Bell rang out from the neighbouring Church-steeple, as the people were entering the Church, Ned met Alice and her husband at the door, availing himself thus of the first opportunity he could obtain to tell his dear "*Miss* Alice" how sincerely he hoped she and her husband would always be as happy as could be. And when they both thanked him, and shook him by the hand, he could not refrain from adding, "And I can't help being glad you've been married within the sound of the Christmas Bells; and I hope their message will be to you all it has been to me, and make you both as happy as it has made me."

After her marriage Ned still continued in the service of his old mistress, and was employed at the school. When Christmas-day next came round, there was another wedding in the little village Chapel. Ned and Jessie Simpson having taken the Bells' advice, "Love one another," took Alice's counsel and were married, and settled in a little ivy-grown cottage that stood in one corner of the grounds belonging to the school, and there they have lived ever since.

And now Ned is getting on in years, and his greatest delight in the whole year is to gather his wife and children, and his mistress with her children, around him in his pretty little home, when Christmas-day comes round, and ask them to listen to the Bells. To his ears their message has never changed since his boyish days of poverty and wretchedness; but as his life, in its varying scenes of happiness and prosperity, interspersed with occasional seasons of sorrow and gloom, has flowed, in the main, pretty evenly on, his experience has confirmed the truth and wisdom of the language of their Song.

"But I have thought, sometimes, that the message has grown a little longer than it was of old," says Ned. "Listen again to the Bells! Can't you fancy they are saying—

"Love one another!
Jesus loves you;
Love one another!
Love Jesus too!
He'll bless you, and keep you!
He'll never forsake you!
Through this life He'll lead you,
Then Home He will take you,
If Him for your Friend and your Saviour you'll take."

"And I'm sure my Jessie and I can say, that our lives have indeed shown that it does, indeed, come true."

This invariably brings a request on the part of the children that old Ned will tell them once again his Story of the Christmas Bells; and gladly does he comply with their wishes. And he always closes it with the Song of the Bells, which has never lost its old charm for him, and never will—

"Love one another!
Jesus loves you;
Love one another!
Love Jesus too!"

"So you'll all have, my dear ones, what old Ned wishes heartily for you all—'A Happy, Merry Christmas!'"

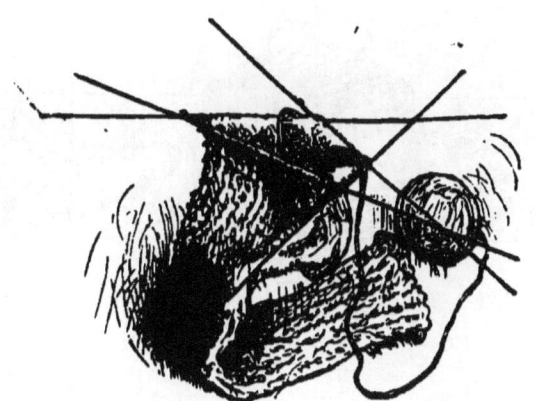

HOW THE UMBRELLA RAN AWAY WITH ELLIE.

HE old clock in the market-place rang out the hour of three, in tones sweet and tremulous with age. The children coming from school counted the strokes, and rejoiced; for when the black, spidery pointers should have thrice again travelled around their dial, Christmas-eve would be begun.

The afternoon is crisp and cool. Jets of thin, bluish smoke curl from the chimneys, like long fingers, all pointing the same way,—pointing to the fir-clad hill which rises beyond the town. If we follow their direction, we should find ourselves on the steep path which crosses its top, and, winding down the other side, runs close to the door of a small cottage, the cottage of Dame Ursula and her little Ellie.

A tiny place,—so low and brown, and hidden among the mossy rocks, that we might pass by without seeing it. In summer there are bee-hives, and the bees buzz cheerfully among the wild thyme; but now their music is frozen into winter silence. And the porch where Ellie sat at her spinning during the sweet, warm days is empty. Only the faint grey curl from the chimney tells of life within.

The door is on the latch. Let us push it open. A few sticks on the hearth, the clock ticking, that is all. No; one other sound, a sigh from the bed in the corner. It is Dame Ursula lying there alone. Poor woman! something very sad has happened.

She has always been so strong and active that she forgot she was no longer young, and climbed up a ladder to mend the thatch on her roof. And she fell, and twisted and bruised her back dreadfully. It hurts her a great deal. She cannot move or work; and here is Christmas at hand, and all her plans for giving Ellie a treat are spoiled. No wonder she sighs.

We came in so softly that she did not hear us; but now the door is pushed open again, and she looks up. It is Ellie, all flushed and rosy, and dragging a great spruce-bough, fresh from the forest. She claps her hands joyously as she cries: "See, Grandmother, here is our Christmas tree."

"Poor child, thou hast nothing to put on it."

"Ah! but this is not all," cries Ellie, again clapping her hands. "I've thought of a plan,—such a plan, Grandmother!"

"And what is that, my Ellie?"

"Thou knowest the silver thaler in the stocking we said should go for the candles and the plums for the Christmas *fête*, my Grandmother?"

"Yes, *liebchen*; but I cannot go to town to buy them."

"But I can, Grandmother,—that is my good plan! I will trim the fire, and set the soup beside thee, before I go. I know the way so well, and the shop with the great fir-tree in the window, and I shall say: 'I am Dame Ursula's little Ellie, and thou must sell me a good measure of plums, because my Grandmother has hurt her back!' And when I return, we will light the candles and hang the raisins and filberts on the bough, and it will be so gay. Dear Grandmother, *do* say I may go."

She looked so eager that the Dame had not the heart to refuse her. She thought of the long distance and the lonely path; but she knew the little feet were light and active, and the little head as wise as a woman's. So she kissed the bright cheek, and answered:—

"Yes, *liebchen*, thou mayest go. Put

on thy Sunday kirtle, and thy red cap, and make thyself neat, as soon as may be, and do not linger upon the road, lest night overtake thee."

Ellie was soon dressed. The fire was stirred, the broth prepared, the little basket reached from its nail.

"And take the umbrella with thee, dear. The winter days often cheat us with rain, and I would not have thee wet," said the Grandmother, last of all.

Now, to be trusted with the umbrella was counted by Ellie a great honour. She willingly obeyed. It had been her Grandfather's, and was very big and blue, with his name cut upon a horn shield on the handle. It was taller than she, and not easy to carry; but she felt proud of it, as, mounting the hill, basket in hand, she went, looking very like Red Riding-Hood, and full of happy thoughts.

The town was safely reached, the errands done. Every one was in holiday humour, and gave full measure to the bright-eyed little maid. Jan, the fruit-merchant, even tucked a gift into her hand—a bright, rosy-cheeked apple. The plums, the tapers, the bit of beef, the filberts, were all stored safely in the basket; but time had flown, and it was nearly six before the heavy-laden little messenger was ready to turn her steps toward home.

The pleasant day was changing into a wild, gusty evening. Little, dull red fragments of sunset were scudding over the sky, and a strong, chill wind piped through the mountain-pass. It blew Ellie along, and was of use in that way; but her fingers grew cold and stiff, and she could hardly hold the basket. At last she hung it on her arm, and just then a few heavy drops fell, and, mindful of Grandmother's order, she put up the umbrella.

Alas for Ellie! As well might a lamb have attempted to manage a balloon at full sail. The umbrella took matters into its own hands at once. It pulled, it flapped, it tore along with the wind, Ellie holding fast the handle. It raced down the hill at full speed, as if bewitched, carrying her with it. First her cap blew off, then the ribbon that bound her hair. The long curls blew into her eyes. Blinded, confused, but never letting go, she lost her breath, and was just beginning to cry, when, before she knew her danger, the umbrella finished by twisting her sharply to one side, and over the edge of a low ravine full of trees. She felt herself falling, felt the umbrella snatched from her grasp, and then she knew no more. All the world grew dark, and she lay as if asleep.

It was long before she woke. When she did, her head and limbs felt heavy and ached. She did not know where she was. Where were the basket and umbrella? Gone, quite gone, and it was dark, and the wind blew loudly in the trees overhead. Was not that enough to make a little girl feel frightened?

She sat up after awhile, and then she saw a light twinkling from a little hollow just below. It was bright and winking, like a million of little tapers, or a whole roomful of glow-worms; and she thought she would creep forward, and find out what it was.

She did so. Such a wonderful sight she had never seen before. The hollow was lined like a nest with green and brown moss and soft yellow grasses. It was so light that she could see every blade, and the little fiery points of the cup-mosses; and the light came from torches, each about the size of a pin, worn in the caps of myriads and myriads of tiny fays, who were flying to and fro, and chattering and clustering together like a swarm of bees. Thousands and thousands of them, and every moment more came,—from nowhere in particular that Ellie could see. They just appeared and took their part in the general hubbub.

But by far the greatest stir was going on about a mossy nook at a little distance, where sat three old men. Great pine-torches were stuck into the trees above their heads, and showed them plainly. One had a seat a little higher than the others, and was taller and more dignified.

His face was sweet and solemn, and looked at least a thousand years old, but his eyes had all the fire of youth, and seemed never to have been weary or ever shed a tear. The other two were stout and furry, with snow-white beards, and faces pink and round like a school-boy's. One wore a queer Dutch roundabout, trimmed with lamb's wool. The other had a vast fur-lined wrapper. Both carried pointed caps on their heads, from under which their little eyes twinkled brightly. Around them on the ground lay heaps and heaps of things,—clothes, books, sugar-plums, rocking-horses, dolls, drums, whistles, great piles of coal, fat turkeys, smoking hot pies with savoury crusts,—every kind of thing that you can think of! All these they were packing as hard as they could into large furry bags; and, as soon as one was filled, two or three thousand fays would seize and drag it off to a place behind the bushes, from which came now and then the tinkling of bells, and a sound as of animals stamping the ground. Ellie looked very hard, and thought she could make out in the dim light a pair of horns above the bushes, but she was not sure.

But neither the fays, nor the torches, nor even the mysterious sounds, attracted her as did the face of the beautiful old man in the midst. It was so sweet and kind that it seemed impossible to keep away from him. Almost before she knew it she had made a few timid steps forward, and was standing in the middle of the hollow. The fays espied her first. With cries and shrieks of laughter like tipsy bells, they clustered about and drew her gently along till she was close to the larger group. A myriad tiny voices began explaining, but the old man held out his hand, and with a look commanded silence.

"I know all, dear little one," he said. "I heard thy steps in the wood-path, and sent the elves but now to break thy fall. Thou knowest me not, but I know thee. Thou art one of my children. Dost thou not guess my name? I am Father Christmas."

"Oh, yes! dear Father Christmas, I know thee well," cried Ellie, in rapture; and she kissed the hand so aged, yet so unwrinkled.

Father Christmas smiled, well pleased.

"And these are my sons," he went on. "This is Kris Kringle. Thou hast heard of him? He takes my gifts to all the little beloved ones of German land and to the Hollanders. Once, a long time since, he used to carry toys across the sea to the children in England; but it was far to go, and now my son Santa Claus takes that business off his hands. They are good boys both of them, but they are young,— quite young."

"Are they much younger than you?" asked Ellie. "Are you very old, dear Father Christmas?"

"Going on two thousand," replied Father Christmas, with a genial laugh. "But I feel young as ever. Hast thou not something in thy pack for this dear child, Kris Kringle?"

"Yes, indeed," cried the old "boy" at

his side. "See, little one,—this,—and this,—and this," and he held up a doll, a book of beautiful pictures, and a fat goose with his legs tied ready for the spit. "And these stockings are for thy grandmother," he went on, as he huddled them into his bag; "but neither she nor you must have them before the time comes. I shall leave them on my way back from town. Many, many people are waiting for me there."

"And for me," said Santa Claus, "they are getting ready even now in England. The stockings are hung up, and the children have begged to go early to bed that they may wake the sooner. The ringers are collecting in the church towers, and blowing upon their fingers that they may be warm to make the bells peal merrily, and the little American boys and girls are waiting. Soon they too will be tucked up. I must be off."

"And have you done your work, my little ones?" asked Father Christmas.

"We have painted every window in the world with pictures," answered some, "and they are all about Christmas,—crosses and evergreen boughs, and spires, so delicate and beautiful. Now, if people only were not stupid! They will wake up to-morrow and see them, and never guess what is meant. There is a fir-bough on your little pane," nodding to Ellie.

"And I have been round and tucked the children up all over the earth," said another, "and kissed the babies so that they shall sleep like dormice while their mammas trim the nursery. Not one is awake in all the cradles, except one little deformed boy who cannot sleep, and for him I wove such a pretty picture that he is laughing instead of crying."

"And I," said another, "have been to visit the crocuses, who are asleep in the cold ground. They roused a little and smiled when I told them what the season was; and I promised if they would be patient and slumber yet a while longer that I would return and awaken them in the spring."

"And I," cried an elf, who seemed to

brim over with frolic and mischief as a flower-cup with dew, "I have been tickling the noses and pulling the wigs of the rich men who sent no turkeys to the poor. 'What, gnats so late in the season!' cried one, and gave his ear a great slap, while another said, 'Phew! it is indeed stinging cold!' Ho!" cried the elf, "stinging cold!"

"And I," said a fifth, "have been distributing the dreams. To the sad, sweet ones; to the sick, peaceful ones; bright and frolicsome ones to all the children. And to good boys and girls I gave the dream of Christmas."

"And I have visited all the poor," whispered another, "and trimmed their dull fires and put sugar in their cups, and above their doors a leaf of the plant called 'Hope.' Have I done well, O my Father?"

"All have done well," said Father Christmas. "And now the clock strikes ten. We must be upon our journey. Harness the reindeer, my elves, and make all ready;

but first this dear child must be safely set upon her homeward way."

The fays bustled about her brightly. Fifty-four of them brought each a raisin from the scattered parcel, others hunted for the basket, while a fatigue party of eight carefully rolled the big red apple into it. Myriads more pursued and found the umbrella, which had stuck fast in a furze-bush. Father Christmas gave his blessing; and aided and helped, she knew not how, by a million tiny fingers, she found herself again on the top of the bank whence she had fallen, her basket on her arm, and the big umbrella in her hand.

The wind had died away, and the moon shone clear. Lightly she tripped down the path and rattled at the latch of the cottage. Poor Dame Ursula had passed a wretched evening listening to the rain, fearing all sorts of evils for Ellie, and weeping over the helplessness which kept her from going to her aid. She had just fallen into a troubled sleep when in danced Ellie, with cheeks like roses, and eyes bright with happy excitement. She threw herself into her grandmother's arms.

"Oh, Grandmother!" she cried, "I have such things to tell thee! Such a wonderful story!"

And Granny listened to the tale with utter bewilderment. Of only one thing she felt sure, she had her darling safe at home again. That was enough to complete her wishes. It was too late for the Christmas tree, but they had it next day. The first thing in the morning Ellie looked at the pane. Yes, there was the fir-bough, the fairy favour, drawn in lines of silvery frost. And at noon came the pastor's wife. She bore in her arms a doll. Her little daughter had sent it, she said. There was a picture book, too. Ellie laughed with glee. She had seen both before. Later in the day their neighbour, the farmer's wife, who did so much for them, made her appearance.

"I have brought you a goose, Dame," she said. "I hope it is a good one. And these stockings are my own knitting.

Don't be discouraged about your fall. It's a long lane that has no turning, you know, and soon you will be up again."

Ellie kissed the kind hand that brought these good things. In her heart she knew that they were not her gift only, but the gift of Christmas.

And that evening, when the spruce-bough twinkled with its tapers, and the raisins and nuts hung beneath them, when the fire blazed its cheeriest, and Grandmother in her new stockings was raised a little in bed, that she might see the savoury goose hissing and bubbling in the pan, Ellie crept away into the corner of the kitchen and patted the big umbrella with a loving hand.

"If you hadn't run away with me," she said, "I should never have seen it all."

JACK'S CHRISTMAS.

JACK had just heard of Christmas for the first time! Ten years old, and never knew about Christmas before! Jack's mother was a weary, overworked woman, and had no heart to tell the children about merry times and beautiful things in which they could have no share.

His parents were very poor and lived in a little cottage by the roadside. This was nice enough in summer, but in winter the house was very cold and bare; the snow drifted through the cracks in the window frame. It was so cold down-stairs that the gravy froze on the children's plates while they were eating breakfast. Mrs. Boyd, Jack's mother, generally went about her work with a shawl tied around her, and a comforter over her ears, on account of the ear-ache; and on the coldest days she kept Jack's little sisters wrapped up from head to foot and perched on chairs near the fire, so they wouldn't freeze. No; she didn't feel much like telling them about Christmas, when she didn't know but they would freeze to death, or, maybe, starve, before that time. But Jack found out. He was going to school that winter, and one learns so much at school! He came home one night brimful of the news that Christmas would be there in three weeks, and that Santa Claus would come down chimneys and say, "I wish you Merry Christmas!" and then put lots of nice things in all the stockings.

Mrs. Boyd heard him talking, and was glad the children were enjoying themselves, but hoped from her heart that they wouldn't expect anything, only to be bitterly disappointed. Most of that evening little Janie, the youngest girl, sat singing,—

> "Wis' you Melly Kitsmas!
> Wis' you Melly Kitsmas!"

in a quaint little minor key, that wasn't plaintive enough to be sad, nor merry enough to be jolly, but only a sweet monotony of sounds and words showing that she was contented, and didn't feel any of the dreadful aches and pains which sometimes distressed her so.

For a week, Jack wondered and mused within himself how he could get something for Christmas presents for his little sisters. He couldn't make anything at home without their seeing it, nor at school without the teacher's seeing it, or else the big boys plaguing him about it. Besides, he would rather buy something pretty, such as they had never seen before—china dolls in pink dresses, or something of that kind. One morning, however, Jack discovered some rabbit marks in the snow near the straw-stack, and he no longer wondered about ways and means, but in a moment was awake to the importance of this discovery. That very evening he made a snare, and the next morning early set it near the stack, and laid an inviting train of wheat quite up to it. He told his sisters, Mary and Janey, about the trap, but not about what he meant to do with the rabbits when he caught them. That afternoon Jack went to his trap, and to his unbounded joy found an imprisoned bunny, frozen quite stiff. He quickly set the trap again, and ran to the house with his capture. All that evening he worked at snares and traps and made three more.

It was so much warmer that their mother let the children stay up a little later than usual; and Mary ventured to bring out her playthings and Janie's. These were two dolls, some bits of broken dishes, and a few little pine blocks. Mary watched her mother's face until she was sure she was "feeling good," before she ventured to begin a play, because on days when mother was very discouraged, it made her feel worse if the children were noisy, and so they would keep quiet and speak in whispers.

"Does Santa Claus bring dolls?" asked Mary, suddenly, of Jack.

"Oh, yes; dolls with pretty dresses on; and little bunnits and pink shoes; and little cubberds to keep their clothes in, and chairs, and everything," said Jack, enthusiastically.

"Oh, my!" sighed Mary, as she looked dolefully at their poor little heap of toys.

Their dolls were old rags, with square pieces of calico tied around them for dresses; and after hearing what Jack said, it wasn't so much fun playing, and the little girls soon went to bed. After they were asleep, Mrs. Boyd said, reproachfully:

"Jack, I wish you wouldn't say anything more about Christmas to the children."

"Why, is it bad?" asked Jack, so astonished that he stopped working.

"No, of course not; but you're getting their heads full of notions about fine things they never can have."

Jack's eyes twinkled.

"Oh, but you don't understand, mother," said he; "may be Santa Claus will come this year."

His mother shook her head.

"You know I caught a rabbit to-day?" whispered Jack.

"Well!" said his mother.

"Well, I'm going to save 'em all the week, and Saturday take 'em to the meatman in the village. I think he'll buy 'em. I heard that he gives threepence each for rabbits. And I'm going to get enough money to buy the girls something nice, and you must make 'em hang up their stockings, mother, and then we'll put the things in after they get asleep."

His mother smiled quite cheerfully.

"Well," said she, "do the best you can."

Their father was away that evening. He was generally away evenings, because most of the neighbours had cosier firesides than his, besides apples, and sometimes cider; and so he passed many a pleasant hour in gossip and farm-talk, while his own little family shivered gloomily at home.

By Saturday morning Jack had three rabbits. The four traps had not been as fruitful as they ought to have been, perhaps, but this was doing very well, and he trudged joyfully to town with his game hanging on a stick over his shoulder. The meat-man did indeed give threepence apiece for his rabbits, and he invited Jack to bring as many more as he could get.

The next Saturday was only two days before Christmas, and how beautiful were all the stores on the village street! Even the groceries had Christmas toys and Christmas trees. A good many boys and girls stood around the shop windows pointing out the things they most admired, and wondering what Santa Claus would bring them. Jack had five more rabbits, which brought him 1s. 3d.; so he was now the owner of two shillings, which was more money than he had ever possessed in all his life before. But when two dolls were bought, and they weren't very fine dolls either, there was only one shilling left. Jack *did* mean to buy something for his mother too, but he had to give that up, and after looking over the bright coloured toy-books in the showcase, he selected two little primers, one with a pink cover and one with a blue one; and, with a big ache in his throat, parted with his last sixpence for sweets. How very, very little he was buying after all, and not one thing for his dear mother who had sat up till two o'clock the night before, mending his ragged clothes for him.

Jack's heart was very heavy as he walked out of the gay shop with such a little package, but it sank still lower when his father's tall form loomed up suddenly before him right in front of the door.

"What are you doing here?" he asked, sternly.

"Been buying a few things," said Jack.

"Let me see 'em," said his father.

Jack tremblingly opened his package.

"Where'd you get the money?"

"With rabbits," said Jack, meekly.

His father fumbled over the things with his big, mittened hand, and said quite gently: "For the girls, I s'pose."

"Yes," answered Jack, beginning to feel relieved.

"Well, run along home."

Jack was only too happy to do so. There wasn't much sympathy between him and his father, nor, indeed, between his father and any of the family—that is, there didn't seem to be; but I think the stream was frozen over, and only needed a few gleams of sunshine to make it bubble on, laughing and gurgling as in the best of hearts.

Jack related his adventures to his mother in whispers, and hid the Christmas articles in the wash-boiler until such time as they should be wanted for certain small stockings. He told his mother how sorry he was not to have a present for her, and that little speech went a long way toward making her happy. That night she sat up —I wouldn't dare tell you how late— making cookies,—something that hadn't been in the house before that winter. She cut them out in all manner of shapes that feminine ingenuity and a knife could compass, not forgetting a bird for Jane, with a remarkably plump bill, and a little girl for Mary, with the toes turned out. She also made some balls of brown sugar (the Boyds never thought of such a luxury as white sugar), to make believe toffee, for she didn't know Jack had bought any.

Now I am going to tell what Mr. Boyd did after he met Jack by the toy-shop. He had gone to the village to have a "good time." That didn't mean, as it does with some men, to get tipsy; but it meant he was going to Munger's shop, where he could meet people, and talk and joke, and keep warm.

Mr. Boyd had been chopping wood for a farmer, and had received his pay; but instead of going dutifully home and consulting with his wife about what he should buy, he was going to "look around" and see what Munger had. He was touched at the sight of Jack's poor little package of gifts, but I doubt if it would have made much impression on his mind if somebody hadn't walked in to Munger's and asked in a brisk, loud voice: "Got any nuts, Munger?"

The man with the brisk voice bought I don't know how many quarts of Brazil nuts and walnuts, and filberts, and almonds, with all the loungers looking on, very much interested in the spectacle. Then he bought raisins, and sweets, and oranges, Mr. Munger growing more smiling every minute.

"Going to keep Christmas, I 'spose," said he, rubbing his hands together.

"That I am; 'Christmas comes but once a year,' and there are little folks up at our house who've been looking for it with all their eyes for a fortnight."

Then he bought a bushel of apples, and, filling a peck measure with them, passed them round among the men who sat and stood about the stove.

"Take 'em home to your little folks if you don't want 'em," he said, when any one hesitated.

There were three or four apples apiece, and Mr. Boyd put all his in his pockets, with a slight feeling of Christmas warmth beginning to thaw his heart.

After this cheery purchaser had gone, some one asked: "Who is that chap?"

"He's the new superintendent of the Orphant Asylum," answered Mr. Munger, rubbing his hands again; "and a mighty nice man he is, too. Pays for all them things out of his own pocket. Very fond of children. Always likes to see 'em happy."

There were two or three men around

that stove who hung their heads, and Mr. Boyd was one of them. He hung his the lowest, perhaps because he had the longest neck. I don't know what the other men did,—something good and pleasant, I hope,—but Mr. Boyd thought

and thought. First he thought how the "orphants" were going to have a brighter and merrier Christmas than his own children, who had both father and mother. Then he thought about sweet, patient little Janie, and quiet Mary, and generous Jack, who had taken so much pains to give pleasure to his sisters, and a great rush of shame filled his heart. Now, when Mr. Boyd was once thoroughly aroused, he was alive through the whole of his long frame. He thumped his knee with his fist, then arose and walked to the counter, where he dealt out rapid orders to the astonished grocer for nuts, candies, and oranges; not in such large quantities, to be sure, as the "orphants'" friend had done, but generous enough for three children. And he bought a calico dress for his wife, a pair of shoes for each of the little girls, and a cap for Jack. That shop contained everything, from grindstones to slate-pencils, and from paraffin to peppermint-drops. These purchases, together with some needful groceries, took all Mr. Boyd's money, except a few pennies; but a Christmas don't-care feeling pervaded his being, and he borrowed a bag, into which he stowed his goods, and set out for home.

It was a pretty heavy bagful, but its heaviness only made Mr. Boyd's heart the lighter. When he reached home, he stood the bag up in one corner, as if it held turnips, and said, "Don't meddle with that, children." Then he went out and spent the rest of the short day in chopping wood, which was very cheering to his wife. So many Sundays had dawned with just wood enough to cook breakfast, that Mrs. Boyd began to dread that day particularly, for her husband was almost sure to go right away after breakfast and spend the whole day at the neighbours' houses, while his own family shivered around a half-empty grate.

Mr. Boyd said never a word about the bag, and the unsuspecting household thought it contained corn or some other uninteresting vegetable, and paid little attention to it. It also stood there all the next day, and the children grew quite used to the sight of it.

Sunday went by quietly, and, to the surprise of all, Mr. Boyd stayed at home, making it his especial business to hold Janie on his lap, and keep the grate well filled with wood. Janie wasn't feeling well that day, and this unusual attention to her made the family very kindly disposed towards their father, whom of late they had come to regard almost as an alien.

Jack, whose shoes were not yet worn out, went to Sunday-school, and after his return the winter day was soon gone. Then he began to fidget, and was very desirous that his mother should put the little girls to bed, while strange to say, his father was desirous that the whole family should go to bed, except himself. In course of time the little girls were asleep in their trundle bed, with their little red stockings hanging behind the door. Mr. Boyd sat with his back to the door, so Jack slipped in his presents without his father's seeing him, and went to his cold bed upstairs.

"Ain't you going to hang up your stocking, mother?" asked Mr. Boyd after Jack had gone.

Mrs. Boyd looked startled.

"Why, no," she answered, hesitatingly, not knowing whether the question was asked in irony or in earnest.

"You'd better," said Mr. Boyd, going to the bag in the corner, and beginning to untie the strings.

He laid out package after package on the floor. His wife knelt down by them in a maze of astonishment. Then, with a great deal of enjoyment, Mr. Boyd untied them one by one, showing candy, nuts, oranges, shoes, and all the rest, except the calico dress, which he kept out of sight.

Aladdin felt very fine when he found the cave-ful of precious stones, but I don't believe he was much happier than Mrs. Boyd. Her eyes were so full of tears that there seemed to be about eight pairs of shoes, ten bags, and half a dozen Mr. Boyds; but she managed to lay hands on the real one, and him she embraced fervently. Then she brought out the cookies and sugar-balls she had made, and said to her husband in a very shame-faced way:

"See my poor presents; I didn't know the children would have anything nice, and I made these. I won't put 'em in their stockings though, now."

But Mr. Boyd insisted on their going in with the other things, and I think they were prized by the children a little more dearly, if such a thing could be possible, than those which they called their "boughten" presents.

Now, I can't begin to describe the joyful time they had the next morning, and particularly, the utter astonishment of Jack, who didn't expect a thing, and hadn't even hung up a stocking. When that devoted boy recognised one of his own gray socks crammed full of knobs and bunches, with a beautiful plush cap on top, he was almost out of his wits. Likewise, Mrs. Boyd's surprise was great at the discovery of her new dress. The little girls were too happy that day to do much else but count and arrange and re-arrange their delightful Christmas presents.

Mr. Boyd killed a chicken, and Jack

contributed a rabbit which he had caught since market-day, and the festival of Christmas was kept with much hilarity by the Boyd family.

The neighbours, one by one, were surprised that Mr. Boyd hadn't dropped in, as he usually did on Sundays and holidays. But Mr. Boyd was engaged elsewhere. And this was only the beginning of good days for that family, for, somehow, the Christmas feeling seemed to last through all the year with Mr. Boyd, and through many other years; and the little ball set rolling by Jack with his rabbit traps, grew to be a mighty globe of happiness for the whole family.

NO POCKET.

IT was at Katie McPherson's Christmas party that the announcement was made, in the dining-room, where the scores of bright children were assembled to partake of the good things which Mrs. McPherson had bountifully provided—Jimmy Johnson made the announcement, and this it was:—

"Bushy Caruthers ain't got no pocket!"

Jimmy delivered this in such tones and with such a manner as he might have used if he had said: "Bushy Caruthers ain't got no thumbs!" or Bushy Caruthers ain't got no nose!"

"Hasn't he?" said Bobby Smedley, with as much eager concern as Jimmy Johnson, or indeed, the most exacting news-bearer, could have asked or desired.

"Hasn't he?" said also Dickey Simpkins.

There was that in Dickey's tone which added, "I'm glad I'm not in Bushy's trousers."

Nellie Partridge, who was one of Jimmy Johnson's audience, opened her eyes roundly and puckered her mouth into a perfect O, and then gave vent to a long "W-h-y!" of astonishment.

"No, he ain't got no pocket," Jimmy repeated, with no abatement in his can-you-believe-it manner.

"That's 'cause he's a little boy," said Tommy Mayneer, who was large of his age.

With this explanation, Tommy thrust his hands into his trousers' pockets, drew himself up to the full capacity of his inches, and marched back and forth a few paces with great dignity.

Nellie Partridge, who, I much fear, will in time grow to be a gossip, hurried over to the group of children in the next corner, and repeated, with solemn eyes,—

"I say! Bushy Caruthers ain't got no pocket!"

"Did you ever?" said one little auditor. "It's too bad," said another. "Why!" exclaimed a third, hurrying away to carry the story to the next group of children. Then the word went to the company of little folks collected at the window; thence to the children outside the dining-room door in the hall, on and on, until everybody knew that Bushy Caruthers was so unfortunate as to be at a party where sweets, and nuts, and oranges, and all manner of good things abounded, and where there was a Christmas-tree, and yet to have no pocket.

What made it worse was, that it was Mrs. McPherson's way at her Katie's Christmas parties, always to insist upon each little guest filling his or her pockets with good things to "take home."

Poor Bushy!

After awhile the word reached Bushy himself. Of course he knew he hadn't any pocket before the children flocked around him with their expressions of condolence and their eager inquiries and exclamations of concern; but until he had heard these, and seen the consternation in the little faces, he had no conception of the magnitude of his misfortune. When this really dawned upon Bushy, he thought he ought to cry; but that seemed too much like baby-conduct. So he perked up his head with an heroic look in his funny little face, and rolled his eyes from one to another of his condolers, as if he would say, "Well, if I ain't got any pocket, I'm going to bear my trouble like a man."

"Well, Bushy," Barney Williamson advised,—" you eat all the candy and jelly and nuts and cake and oranges you can hold."

" What makes um call you Bushy, anyhow?" asked Henry Clay Martin. "You ain't bushy a bit; you're smooth as my black-and-tan terrier;" and Henry Clay looked the unfortunate over from the crown of his glossy black head to the soles of his polished gaiters.

"My name's Bushrod, and they call me Bushy for short," was the explanation; whereupon a dozen or more children proceeded to tell what their right names were and what they were called for short.

Meantime Bushy, in accordance with Barney Williamson's advice was engaged in storing away cakes and candies, regardless of headaches and doctors. At the end of fifteen minutes he had probably discovered the limit of his capacity; for at this time he went over to his papa with both hands full of bon-bons, and emptied them in that gentleman's big coat-pocket; and when papa looked behind him for an explanation of the pullings, and so on, Bushy said, pathetically:

"I ain't got no pocket, papa."

"You *have* no pocket, you mean," corrected papa, gently.

"Yes, papa, I haven't no pocket.

In a few moments he was back again, and papa felt another tugging at his coat behind, and heard something rattling down into his pocket; again came the explanation from Bushy; "I ain't got no pocket, papa."

It was not long after this before the folds of mamma's silk dress were disturbed, and down on the top of her handkerchief streamed the sweets and nuts from Bushy's overflowing hands, attended by the inevitable explanation: "I ain't got no pocket, mamma. Katie says we must all take home something."

Again and again was the silk-dress pocket visited, for it was roomy, and mamma, busy in conversation, was unconscious of the visitations.

Then Bushy's sister, Minnie, thirteen years old, was petitioned to lend the aid of her pocket to the pocketless boy. Beside this, Bobby Smedley, whose home was just across the street from Bushy's, volunteered the loan of one-quarter of one of his pockets for the transportation of Bushy's nick-nacs.

Mary Endicott, who lived next door to the unfortunate boy, hearing of Bobby Smedley's generosity, forthwith devoted a half of her roomy pocket to Bushy's relief.

But it was when the children had gone upstairs to the parlour where the Christmas tree stood, that Bushy's concern attained its height.

"S'pose," he said to Barney Williamson, remembering Barney's *rôle* as adviser, "s'pose I was to get a great lot of things —that ball"—and he pointed to the spangled, radiant tree, with its wonderful blossoms and fruit—"and that top, and that drum, and that trumpet, with a whistle, and, oh! them two wrasling niggers, and that whistle, and that cannon, and that velocipede, and that engine, and that there wheelbarrow, and a great lot more, how could I get them all home?—'cause I ain't got no pocket, you know."

"Well I'll tell you," said the ready Barney. "I'll pack all the other things in your wheelbarrow, you know, and roll 'em home for you."

Bushy did get the wheel-barrow, sure enough, and soon had it loaded up.

You may well believe there was laughing at Bushy's house when all the pockets were emptied, and all the boxes and baskets and the overflowing wheelbarrow. Such heaps of candy! such piles of cakes! such quantities of almonds and raisins, mottoes, lady-apples, oranges, and other good things, as were displayed! In Bushy's eagerness he had actually smuggled a chicken's wing and buttered biscuit into his mother's keeping. There was enough, as he said, ecstatically, for another party.

If he had gone to Katie's entertainment with pockets all over his chubby little form, he could not have fared so well.

"Mamma," said Bushy, gravely, as he cracked an almond between his white teeth, his black eyes, meanwhile, sweeping the table which held his collection of sweets, "don't never put no pocket in my party-trousers."

www.ingramcontent.com/pod-product-compliance
Lightning Source LLC
Chambersburg PA
CBHW020120170426
43199CB00009B/572